First Day on the Ice:
Tips from a Professional Skating Coach (and Mom)

Jocelyn Jane Cox

March '18

Enjoy!

To my mother, Barbara, for getting me my first pair of skates, the pink pompoms to put on them, and for always kindly encouraging me... as a skater, a coach, and a writer.

Table of Contents

Introduction

If you're thinking about taking your child Ice Skating for the first time and you're feeling a little nervous (or: completely freaked out!) about it, this book is designed to help make it a smooth process and a positive experience for both you and your child. You don't have to have any skating skills yourself or any background on the ice in order to get your child started with basic skating skills that can lead to participating in figure skating, ice hockey, or speed skating.

I was a competitive figure skater for 11 years and was on the U.S. National Team when I was a teenager. In the last 25 years, I've coached hundreds of kids, from beginners to elite figure skaters, but getting my own young son out on the ice recently has helped me to see this process from the other side. For one thing, I *now* realize that merely getting a young child out the front door and into the car on any day of the week is a major triumph. But I've also started to understand the importance of a few key details, and specifically what we can do as parents to make the first attempts at skating more enjoyable...and lead to more fun on the ice.

1. Why Ice Skating?

Ice Skating is not only a great form of exercise, it can be an excellent source of confidence for kids who end up loving it. Regardless of talent and aptitude, skating is a way to build muscle and cardiovascular strength, improve coordination, and increase the mind-body connection.

For little ones, it's a perfect environment to learn through play. From the very beginning, this activity touches on concepts such as fast-slow, stop-go, up-down. We skate in circles, skate in straight lines, and skate in zigzags. Besides, children can see that listening and following directions produces immediate physical results. As in: *Oh wow, what the teacher said works. I'm moving!*

The ice rink is chock full of larger life lessons, too. We're talking about things like perseverance and good sportsmanship. My personal favorite lesson is: getting up after a fall. I mean this in the literal sense, but also more generally, in the form of recovering from setbacks.

What I learned as a figure skater (and later, playing ice hockey in college) has helped me in all aspects of my life. Skating helped me understand how to set short- and long-term goals and manage performance anxiety. In my career as a coach, I have seen it influence my skating students in similar ways – I think all of us draw strength from our years on the ice.

Granted, life skills can (and should!) be obtained through many sports and activities, but I think ice sports combine a unique "balance" of:
• cognition and emotion
• finesse and physical aggressiveness
• self-control and freedom

Skating can help your children acclimate to other sports as well. For example, after a few months of regular skating, your kids will take to skiing like fish jumping into water.

It's a great skill for our kids to have in their back pockets in case they get invited to skating birthday parties or skating play dates. And it's just a fun, active, thing to do on a recreational basis all year long. In the winter, when playgrounds in many parts of our country are covered in snow, many of us are desperate to find alternative ways for our kids to burn off some of that energy – the rink is an ideal place to do this.

In the summer, it's a perfect way to beat the heat. Most indoor rinks in the U.S. are open all year long. I love my job in every season, but walking into my chilly workplace when the temperatures are soaring is actually refreshing.

Finally, skating is a lifelong sport that your children will be able to enjoy with *their* own children some day.

2. When to Start

Many of the athletes we see on television during the Winter Olympics stepped on the ice for the first time before the age of five. Even if you're not looking to head in that direction, exposing kids to skating early is ideal because their center of gravity is low and they don't have far to fall. Besides, it wasn't so long ago that they were falling while learning how to walk...and that generally makes them more fearless than older, taller kids.

This guide is geared toward younger kids, ages 3-6, but of course kids can start at any age and much of the forthcoming information will apply to kids of all ages. Many of these suggestions even apply to adults who want to get out there - Go ahead! It is truly never too late to start. I have taught many beginner (and also accomplished) adult skaters over the years.

I first got on the ice around the age of six on outdoor rinks in Wisconsin, but I didn't start taking lessons at an indoor rink until the age of 8. My older brother, who eventually became ranked 6th in the nation in pair skating, didn't switch over from hockey skates to figure skates and start taking lessons until he was 13. So both of us got what would be considered late starts, for eventual competitors.

I took our son skating when he was still two-years-old; I just couldn't help myself...most coaches can't seem to wait. That first day, we did a lot of sitting on the ice. Mostly, I gave him "taxi rides" around the rink, by bending forward and completely holding him from behind. He enjoyed this immensely, however...my lower back paid the price. I didn't get him in skates again for another year, and by the age of three (almost four), he was far more balanced and ready to stand up a bit more on his own.

My brother has gotten all three of his children on the ice early. His youngest son zips across the ice with remarkable ease, and my brother attributes this to what he calls the "Carpet Roller Skating Method." He put his son in inexpensive plastic roller skates on the carpet at home. Just marching around in those got my nephew accustomed to that unstable feeling, got him adjusting for balance, and also got him used to falling. It's crazy, but because of this, my nephew could pretty much skate without any help when he first stepped on the ice! The beauty of this method is that you can do a very short "skate" of 10 minutes without even leaving the house. This can really make Day One on the ice go smoothly.

3. What to Wear

Like most sports and activities, the right gear is essential. Get your child suited up in the following:
- helmet
- snow pants
- puffy coat
- mittens

You want your child to be warm and also have ample padding for falls. What I learned when I played ice hockey in college is that padding is a game changer. With enough padding, falling can actually be pretty fun!

So that your child is comfortable in the skates, opt for thinner socks, since thick socks tend to bunch up. You also want socks that are long enough to ride above the ankle, perhaps a few inches up onto the shin. Otherwise, the upper edge of the boot could dig into her skin; a subtle situation that the child might not be able to verbally express and that could end the skating attempt before it even begins.

The following note applies no matter where you are: whether you're going for a bike ride or your child is going for a spin on the scooter, don't rush while helping to clasp the straps of the helmet. If you accidentally get some skin pinched in there, like I have, you will not only feel terrible, but your child will emit a scream that could shatter all the windows of the building and perhaps even shatter the ice. Do what you tell your child to do all the time: slow down, concentrate.

Bike helmets are great, but if you want to make the extra investment, and if you're particularly worried about your child's beautiful pearly whites, you can purchase a hockey helmet with the cage in front. Actually, children almost never hit their teeth on the ice, but they do sometimes hit their chins. Ski helmets are also an option.

Speaking of gear, make sure you wear enough warm clothing, yourself, even if you're going to stay on the sidelines. In order to keep that ice frozen, rinks are chilly even in the middle of the summer. In the winter, they can be frigid. I mention this because I know that most of us parents are rushing out the door and thinking mostly about what our kids need for an activity...in the process we forget to think about ourselves.

4. What to Talk About Beforehand

You don't need to belabor the point, but make sure you mention that the ice is going to be slippery, so your child isn't shocked by this fact. This is one of those tidbits that's obvious to us, but three and four-year-olds with no exposure to a rink yet may not realize it. I would mention this in the car on the way to the rink.

Let them know that it might feel a little funny. They're going to be sliding across the ice in special shoes with medal blades on the bottom.

Let them know it's okay to fall. In fact, everybody falls, even the best skaters in the world fall ALL the time. You don't want to scare them, but you can tell them that coaches fall, adults fall, and big kids fall. It's kind of the ice skating version of the iconic potty training book, *Everybody Poops*: Everybody Falls! Some kids will enjoy falling, spinning out, and sliding across the ice. Other kids will be terrified. Others will start off terrified and either gradually or quickly get used to it. Falling is a part of skating. Believe it or not, you *want* your child to fall several times on that first day so that they get used to it.

5. The Skates

If you decide to buy your child her own pair of skates, just know that she'll grow out of them as quickly as she grows out of sneakers and you might not get much use out of them. All rinks provide rental skates for a small fee in addition to the session fee. I recommend this at first. If your child develops an interest in skating, you can always purchase skates down the road.

The person at the rental desk is likely going to give you a choice regarding the blades: figure skates or hockey skates? Whether or not you're hoping to head toward hockey or figure skating, most beginner-level coaches believe it's best to choose figure skates for at least the first few months. Figure skating blades have toe picks, and yes, you can trip over them, but what's good about them is that they're flatter than hockey blades, and therefore more of the blade is on the ice at all times. Hockey blades have more of what is called a "rocker" – like the bottom of a rocking chair – and this can cause a young child to literally rock back and forth and render them unable to find their balance. Most kids don't have the core strength to handle this at first. Truthfully, I recommend the same for beginner adults as well. Trust me, tripping over the toe picks is actually preferable to being a human rocking chair!

The staff member at the rental desk will ask the child's shoe size, but note that you may have to try on a few different sizes of rentals, as they all run a bit differently.

It's a good idea to get to the rink early, maybe 20 minutes before you intend to get on the ice, in order to get the gear all worked out.

To figure out if the size is correct, ask your child if she can wiggle her toes inside the skating boot. Whether the rental skates have standard laces, velcro straps, or plastic pull-straps like ski boots, it's important to make the skates tight around the ankle. Skates are stiffer than sneakers and snow boots, and they aren't supposed to feel super comfy like other footwear. Sometimes I say, "I know these don't exactly feel like your bunny slippers, but that's actually a good thing." You want the skates snug so that they give the child support in the ankles, as opposed to flopping side to side. If your child is resistant to this tighter fit, assure her that this will make it easier to skate and help with balance.

6. Lessons

If you are confident in your skating skills and plan to get on the ice with your child, you can go to what is called a public session. These are open to the general public, as opposed to "freestyle sessions" which are for experienced figure skaters and "stick time," which are for hockey players. Call ahead or check the rink's website to find out when these blocks of time are offered.

However: if it's in the budget, I highly recommend getting a lesson, or lessons, for your child so that a professional can both provide some information and also do the heavy lifting i.e. pick your child up off the ice, if needed!

You can go two different routes with this: group lessons or private lessons on public sessions. It's best to call your local rink to ask some questions before you go. Sometimes rinks can provide a private a coach on the spot, but not always, so it's really best to set it up beforehand.

Group lessons usually run on 8 to 10 week cycles and are more cost-effective than private lessons. Depending on enrollment, i.e. if there is room in the classes, you can usually jump into these at anytime in the series with pro-rated fees. These are great because of the social aspect...your child can be motivated by other kids their age. *Hey that kid is skating across the ice, I guess I can too.* Or maybe it will be more like, *Hey everybody's going over there, so I guess I will too.*

You can also ask about private lessons – these will generally be more expensive, but the one-on-one instruction can be helpful for kids (or parents) who are feeling particularly timid about this. You can take a few private lessons just to get started or you can hire someone indefinitely.

Either way, a professional coach can do things on the ice that parents can't, such as help to hold the child upright without falling themselves. And as, mentioned above, they can help get children back on their feet if they are struggling to do so on their own.

Depending on the rink's rules, coaches sometimes have permission to use magic markers to draw patterns on the ice, like little paths to follow, or little characters. My own drawing skills are...well, questionable, but my son loves this anyway. If I draw a bunch of smiley faces on the ice, he will excitedly skate from one to the other, especially if I give them ridiculous names like Beluga Bill or Sally Sunflowerhead.
Sometimes, coaches even let the children draw on the ice, too, an opportunity that seems to be just crazy enough to seem thrilling – *what? drawing on ice?* Coaches can incorporate plush toys into the lesson, or small construction cones to create obstacle courses. Again, this is all dependent on the rink's rules, the scenario, and the coach's style. The point is that, in addition to providing technical information, coaches have a lot more leeway in making it fun.

Most coaches avoid and recommend avoiding those walkers, or crates, or anything you sometimes see kids pushing along the ice. Children will get the hang of skating far faster without these crutches. Not all rinks even offer these and they're not entirely safe for the other people skating; others could get hurt if they crash into them.

7. Lobbytime: Right Before Getting on the Ice

As mentioned earlier, if you are taking a lesson, get to the rink about 20 minutes early on the first day, in order to get all the layers on, and the skates all set.

The first thing you want to do after getting the skates on is walk around a bit so your child can get accustomed to the skates, and so that you can asses if they are tight enough around the ankles. Take a little tour of the lobby – look at whatever photos, pictures, or signs they have hanging up, and maybe walk over to the bathroom so you know where that is. (Steer clear of the vending machines, video games, and toy machines if you don't want to commit to a purchase...alas... we all know avoiding this is pretty much impossible, sigh.) The point is that a little stroll will start developing the balance in the skates without your child even realizing it.

If you are lucky enough to see the Zamboni, or the "ice truck" as my son first called it, out on the ice, that's a fun thing to go over and watch as well. The Zamboni smoothes the ice with hot water every few hours and kids peer through the plexiglass with fascination. My son even got a wave from the driver, once, and it was pretty much the greatest thing that ever happened to him.

Note that most rink lobbies have rubber flooring throughout, since this is a good surface for the blades. You never want to step directly on the metal bleachers or on the cement outside the front door, as this will ruin the blades, or at least compromise the sharpening and render the blade less able to slide across the ice.

On the first day of skating, one of the main goals is for your child to be able fall and get back up on her feet on her own. Feeling stuck and stranded every time she falls can make the child miserable and frustrated – if they can't figure out how to get back up, I've seen lots of kids crawl in a bee-line for the door and straight off the ice!

Here's how you can help with this: after you get your child's skates on, sit down on the floor with her. Then get to your hands and knees, on all fours, "like a puppy." From there, try to get one foot up, and flat on the floor. Finally, use one hand on your knee and one hand on the floor to push your rear end up into the air, and get the other foot flat on the ground. Try this three times before your child gets on the ice. I hate to say it, but this is probably going to be a lot more challenging for you than it is for your child! Consider this your workout for the day. Many coaches will start the skating class this way, either on or off the ice.

My husband, who is not a skater, learned this lesson the hard way when he proposed to me on the ice at Rockefeller Center. After he got down on bended knee, and I said YES, he needed my help to stand back up again. Needless to say, I was a bit shaky on my own feet, at that point. Apparently he did do one secret practice run of this in the lobby, but he might have benefited from a few more tries!

8. Time to Skate! Or Just Stand or Sit

Obviously, the first day on the ice isn't about spins or triple axels or even...gliding, for that matter. For a young child and first-timer, just standing still on the ice is an achievement. Of course, for a toddler or pre-schooler just standing still anywhere is a huge achievement!

As mentioned earlier, getting back up from the ice is the next goal. I start all my lessons with the littles by falling down first. Yes, I make a big dramatic show out of it, and laugh theatrically, so they see that skating teachers fall, too. Then I take them through the steps of getting back up – *hands and knees like a puppy* – mentioned above. I do this at least three times. Some kids will have no problem and pop right up, and some kids will need assistance.

The next thing is baby steps: literally. Sure, in the future, you want these long, gliding strides called "strokes," but at the beginning it's best to take tiny steps, kind of like marching. Keeping the feet right under the shoulders with small steps makes it easier to balance. Counting these "One, two, one, two!" and asking the kids to do so out loud is usually a hit.

When you first start, you want to keep your weight and your arms a bit forward. This helps to keep your upper body somewhat still, which will help you to glide. I tell the kids to stretch their arms out in front of them like zombies or I have them wiggle their fingers as if they're playing the piano.

Another reason you want to keep your arms and your weight forward is because you want to fall forward, not back. When you fall backwards, there's a higher chance of hitting your head. (Don't forget to wear those helmets as already suggested.) Getting the upper body under control is key for safety; kids and adults whose arms are flailing all over the place have a higher chance of getting hurt, but also less of a chance of actually moving forward across the ice.

Kids and adults alike can "catch a fall," in other words, prevent it from happening, by bending forward and putting their hands on their knees and freezing in that position. Sometimes I call out the word: "FREEZE!" to remind kids to do this when they look like they're about to fall. Actually, this is another great thing to practice in the lobby beforehand.

Safety note: If taking a private or group lesson just isn't in the budget and you are up for getting out there with your child, I recommend *not* holding onto your child's hand, tempting as it may be. If you do have some skating experience and stability, the best thing to do is to hold your child under their armpits, from behind, so that you're both facing the same way; this is how skating coaches do it (as much as it takes a toll on our backs.)

Really, I recommend not holding onto your child at all, even if you do have some confidence, because they can hit your feet or knock you down accidentally, and you don't want to topple on top of your child. While skating is an excellent family activity to share, two unstable people trying to balance together on a slippery surface with sharp blades attached to their feet just isn't a safe undertaking. *Never* pick up your child and carry her in the air on the ice. This is very dangerous and, again, could get you both hurt. Finally, if you are new to the ice, it's a good idea to wear a helmet yourself.

9. Keep it Fun

The most important thing is to keep that first day as playful as possible. After getting all bundled up, ask her something like: *Do you feel like a polar bear?!* After taking a few victorious steps either on the floor or the ice: *Woah! I think there's a penguin with a green helmet out here?!* If your child, like mine, is all about adventure, you can pretend you're embarking on an expedition across an iceberg. The point is, the more like playing this is, the more likely your child is going to enjoy it.

What I'm about to suggest next will take some self-control on your part, but when your child falls, don't wince and freak out. Don't rush over and yell out, OH NO! ARE YOU OKAY?! even if you're shrieking that on the inside. If you smile, laugh, and even clap when your child falls, she's more likely to do the same thing. Usually, falling is more surprising than painful for little ones, so our positive reactions go a long way in helping our kids to see that it's no big deal. Along these lines, if you see the coach reacting to falls in this way, it isn't because she doesn't care about the child's safety, it's because she's trying to downplay the falls.

Likewise, resist the urge to say, "You didn't fall at all!" if this happens to be the case. While staying positive is of course exactly the right instinct, remember that the goal is to get moving, and, as I've mentioned, falling is going to be a part of this. Instead, focus more on distance, and applaud the child for how far she got across the ice even if she fell 76 times along the way (and even if she only made it two feet!). "Wow, look how far you went!"

Most kids are far more resilient than we think, and far more resilient (and limber) than we are. But if the child is crying after a fall, I first make sure they aren't hurt. If not, I ask something silly, like if they tripped over a penguin. *Wait,* [looking around] *where did that penguin go? Did he even say excuse me?* Or I say: *I know the ice is kind of hard. I sure wish it was made out of something softer…like clouds or mattresses…or can you think of anything soft?* In the process of conjuring up marshmallows or cotton candy, they might forget they fell in the first place and even get back up onto their feet without thinking about it.

Just have fun on the first day and don't put any pressure on it. Some kids will take to the ice right away and start gliding joyfully in circles. Some will require several attempts before getting comfortable on that weird, slippery surface. If your child really isn't enjoying the ice, just go back home and try again next week, next month, or next year. It's amazing how much a little bit of growth – both physical and mental development – can help them both control their limbs and understand directions.

Even if you follow all the tips here, don't expect it to go perfectly, don't get discouraged, and, above all else, don't be critical of your child. I've watched countless kids who struggled with their physical coordination at first become gold medalists. I've watched shy, timid kids become beautiful skaters and flourish on the ice. Conversely, I've watched incredibly talented kids not take a real interest in skating, and quit early despite all their potential. Sometimes this is because of parental pressure; other times it's simply because they don't enjoy it enough. So you just never know.

I think, as parents, it's critical to expose our kids to a myriad of healthy activities, so they can find the ones they truly enjoy. Sure, there are going to be rough days in any sport or any activity, and we're going to have to constantly help them through ups and downs, but there's really nothing more gratifying than seeing a child's love for a sport blossom and seeing their own inner-drive kick in. Once you see their abilities and self-confidence start to soar, your heart will surely start to soar, too.

Everything we do, everything we try...starts with a first day. I hope these tips will help your child's first day on the ice to be a positive one and lead to many others to come.

In Summary

- Call your local rink beforehand for session times and lesson information.
- Bring helmet, snow pants, puffy coat, mittens, long-ish socks, and also layers for yourself.
- Talk about the fact that the ice is slippery and that it's okay to fall.
- Make sure you get the skates tight enough around the ankle.
- Practice getting up and down in the skates.
- Have fun!

Acknowledgements

Thank you to my talented husband, Rob Strati, for designing the book cover, for his general support, and for rolling with my weird, early-late coaching schedule. Thank you to my son for going skating with me and helping me to see this process from a whole new perspective. Thank you to my brother Brad Cox, my former skating partner, and now my coaching partner, who is responsible for getting me started in this sport so long ago and keeping me going, throughout *all* the falls. Thank you to my skating students, past and present; I have learned more from them over the years than I could ever possibly express. Thank you to the wonderful coaches I had the benefit of learning from, in Wisconsin, as a beginner, and in Newark, Delaware as a national competitor, with a special thanks to Georgia Roeming, Stacey Smith, Robbie Kaine, and Jill Cosgrove. Thank you to Haley Ruotolo, former student and now colleague, who gave me critical feedback on this manuscript. Thank you to my fellow coaches and the staff at Westchester Skating Academy in Elmsford, NY where I have enjoyed coaching for almost 20 years. Finally, thank you to all my mom friends, including Sara Weiss, who have been asking me about the how-what-whens of skating – you are the inspiration for this book. Thanks for reading these acknowledgements, I realize that they are almost as long as the book itself!

About the Author

Jocelyn Jane Cox is a freelance writer, humorist, and figure skating coach. She was formerly a nationally-ranked competitor in ice dance and pair skating with her brother, Brad Cox, and has been coaching figure skating for over 25 years. She holds an M.F.A. in creative writing from Sarah Lawrence College. Her work has appeared in a wide range of parenting, skating, literary, and humor publications. Her 2012 satirical book, *The Homeowner's Guide to Greatness* was an Amazon bestseller in the humor category. She lives with her husband and young son near Nyack, New York.

Made in the USA
Middletown, DE
06 February 2018